The

Url

Designing for the Future at the Brooklyn Navy Yard

Yale School of Architecture
180 York Street
New Haven, CT 06520
www.architecture.yale.edu

Distributed by Actar
355 Lexington Avenue, 8th fl.
New York, NY 10017
www.actar.com

The Innovative Urban Workplace was made possible
through an endowment from the Edward P. Bass
Distinguished Visiting Fellowship at the Yale School
of Architecture. It is the sixteenth in a series of
publications of the Edward P. Bass Distinguished Visiting
Fellowship published through the dean's office.

Editors: Nina Rappaport and Stella Xu
Design: Manuel Miranda Practice
Copy Editor: Cathryn Drake
Library of Congress Control Number: 2022947608
ISBN: 978-1-63840-080-6

THE INNOVATIVE URBAN WORKPLACE

Designing for the
Future at the
Brooklyn Navy Yard

Abby Hamlin
Dana Tang
Andrei Harwell

The Edward P. Bass
Visiting Distinguished
Architecture Fellowship,
Yale School of Architecture

Edited by
Nina Rappaport
and Stella Xu

CONTENTS

PREFACE

**Edward P. Bass Distinguished
Visiting Architecture Fellowship Dedication**

In 2003 Edward P. Bass, a 1967 graduate of Yale College who graduated from the Yale School of Architecture in 1972, endowed this fellowship for property developers to lead advanced studios in collaboration with design faculty. An environmentalist, Bass sponsored the Biosphere 2 development in Oracle, Arizona, in 1991. As a developer he is contributing to the ongoing revitalization of downtown Fort Worth, Texas, where his project Sundance Square, combining restoration and new construction, has transformed a moribund urban core into a vibrant regional center. In his work Bass has been guided by the conviction that architecture is a socially engaged art operating at the intersection of grand visions and everyday realities.

The Bass fellowship ensures that the school curriculum recognizes the role of property developers as an integral part of the design process by inviting them to work with educators and architecture students in the studio and contextualize the practice of architecture within the wider professional discourse. The following books have been published on the studio projects in the series:

2006
Poetry, Property, and Place
Gerald Hines and Stefan Behnisch

2007
Future Proofing
Stuart Lipton, Richard Rogers, Chris Wise, and Malcolm Smith

2008
The Human City: Kings Cross
Roger Madelin and Demetri Porphyrios

2009
Urban Integration: Bishopsgate Goods Yard
Nick Johnson and FAT Architects

2010
Learning in Las Vegas
Chuck Atwood and David M. Schwarz

2011
Urban Intersections: São Paulo
Katherine Farley and Deborah Berke

2015
Rethinking Chongqing: Mixed Use and Super Dense
Vincent Lo, Paul Katz, Jamie von Klemperer, and Forth Bagley

2015
Social Infrastructure: New York
Douglas Durst and Bjarke Ingles

2016
The Marine Etablissement: New Terrain for Central Amsterdam
Isaäc Kalisvaart, Alexander Garvin, Kevin D. Gray,
and Andrei Harwell

2017
A Sustainable Bodega/Hotel in Rioja
John Spence, Andy Bow, and Patrick Bellew

2017
Paranoazinho: City Making Beyond Brasilia
Rafael Birmann and Sunil Bald

2018
Harlem: Mart 125
Jonathan Rose, Sara Caples, and Everardo Jefferson

2019
...And More
The catalog of an exhibition on Governors Island based on the studio of Michael Samuelian, Simon Hartmann, and Andrei Harwell

2020
The Diamonds of American Cities
Janet Marie Smith, Alan Plattus, and Andrei Harwell

2022
Next Generation Tourism — Touching the Ground Lightly
John Spence, Henry Squire, Patrick Bellew, and Timothy Newton

With this 16th publication in the series it is a pleasure to present the research and studio led by real estate developer Abby Hamlin with architect Dana Tang.

INTRODUCTION

Nina Rappaport and Stella Xu

The Innovative Urban Workplace: Designing for the Future at the *Brooklyn Navy Yard* presents design projects produced by students of the 15th Edward P. Bass Distinguished Visiting Architecture Fellowship studio at the Yale School of Architecture. It was taught by Abby Hamlin, Bass Fellow and founder of Hamlin Ventures; Dana Tang, architect and partner at Gluckman Tang Architects; and Yale School of Architecture faculty member Andrei Harwell.

The studio investigated the role played by the Brooklyn Navy Yard (BNY) in the history of manufacturing in the framework of its mission "to fuel New York City's economic vitality by creating and preserving quality jobs, growing the City's modern industrial sector and its businesses, and connecting the local community with the economic opportunity and resources of the Yard." The conversations, essays, research findings, and projects in this book record a semester of study and analysis around issues of job creation, worker experience, urban equity, and environmental stewardship. The students developed distinctive ideas and solutions that speak to the type of workplace needed in urban sites today. Their projects also reflect ideas about how building design can affect urban job outcomes in a socially and environmentally equitable way.

During the first weeks of the studio, students worked in teams carrying out a series of exercises in research and analysis to frame an understanding of public development on the site. The students also had the opportunity to discuss the issue of urban manufacturing and workplaces with the leadership and master planners of the BNY, local officials and city planners, and technical experts in the fields of urban design and sustainable building technology. During the research phase students reexamined the BNY master plan proposal and explored alternatives for the site's development. The book opens with a design brief outlining the challenges and opportunities facing the studio. This section discusses the role of the Yard in both historical and contemporary contexts. It also contemplates the role of the urban workplace, especially in the post-pandemic era, during which remote work has become increasingly significant. The brief is followed by Nina Rappaport's interview with Abby Hamlin and Dana Tang about their personal and professional experiences, past projects, and views on design and development.

The next section of the book delineates the BNY master plan produced by WXY Architects in 2018. Following are two panel discussions between the students and local officials, city planners, and technical experts including Kate Ascher, Justin Garrett Moore, and Andy Darrell, as well as a second discussion with Nina Rappaport.

The fifth and sixth sections showcase the students' research findings, project concepts, and spatial designs throughout the semester. Assessing the site's physical constraints, neighborhood context, and market parameters, each student developed a distinctive project concept that reinvented a program aiming to reconcile competing elements of the BNY's mission and objectives. Many of the projects systematically identified potential urban business models that address future relationships between places of production and consumption. Students also looked at comparable waterfront development projects and addressed issues including flood mitigation and environmental remediation in their proposals.

The editors would like to recognize the valuable contributions of students in the classes of 2021 and 2022 to the production of this book under the challenging constraints presented by COVID-19: Ives Brown, Xuefeng Du, Niema Jafari, Hyun Jae Jung, Dreama Simeng Lin, Stella Xu, Young Joon Yun, Yuhan Zhang. We also extend our thanks to our copy editor, Cathryn Drake, as well as our graphic designers, Manuel Miranda Practice.

STUDIO BRIEF

Abby Hamlin, Dana Tang, Andrei Harwell

Even before COVID-19 upended the national economy along with work and travel plans, significant forces of change had altered the following spheres of work in New York City: who does the work, how it is performed, and the location and design of the workplace. Traditional manufacturing jobs, which once provided a pathway into the middle class, were relocated offshore or in suburban and exurban settings. Today New York relies on small-scale urban manufacturers and innovative offices in the TAMI (technology, advertising, media, and information) sectors as well as biotechnology, health care, and arts and cultural production to shape its employment future.

The shift in New York's business profile has profoundly affected individuals as well as the economy, exacerbating the unequal distribution of wealth and opportunity among the city's diverse populations. College-educated and professionally trained individuals continue to thrive, while many immigrants and those who lack college degrees, especially individuals of color, struggle to get by with limited educational, career, and economic options.

The Role of the Yard

New York City has attempted to address the impact of lost manufacturing jobs in multiple ways. One approach is providing support for contemporary industrial development in the 300-acre publicly owned Brooklyn Navy Yard (BNY). Situated on the Brooklyn waterfront, it is a nationally recognized model of the successful transformation of an urban industrial site. Established in 1801, the BNY served as America's premier shipbuilding facility for 165 years, until it was decommissioned by the U.S. Navy in 1966 and sold to the city. At its peak, during World War II, the BNY generated more than 70,000 jobs and served as the economic heart of Brooklyn.[1]

1 Lauren Cook, "Brooklyn Navy Yard surpasses 10,000 jobs for 1st Time in Over 50 Years," *AMNY Newsletter,* 2019

Under the stewardship of the nonprofit Brooklyn Navy Yard Development Corporation (BNYDC), the BNY has transitioned from its maritime origins to a contemporary industrial park. Today it is home to a network of more than 450 businesses that generate 10,000 jobs. The city's goal is to see the BNY add 10,000 new jobs by 2030, toward a future total employment goal of 30,000 jobs when the campus is fully built.

Real estate development plays a vital role in the BNY's success. Partnering with developers or developing projects on its own, the BNYDC has redeveloped or contracted to develop more than 40 buildings and 5 million square feet of commercial spaces within its campus. Some of the projects, including New Lab and Steiner Studios, represent innovative state-of-the-art workplaces that set the standard for design in their fields.

Today the BNY has run out of space. To achieve the city's job-creation goals, new buildings must be built and new tenants attracted. However, what type of work space should be built? And how much space is needed? Which business types should the BNY target to have the most beneficial impact on the city's future? Can real estate development alone attract jobs, or are there other potential strategies? How can building design affect the generation of jobs?

To guide future growth, the BNY retained WXY Architects to prepare a master plan calling for the addition of a total of 5.1 million square feet divided among four vacant sites on the campus. The proposed development seeks to create an "ideal mix" of future tenant types at the BNY: 25% traditional manufacturers, 25% innovative manufacturers, 25% producers for the city, 20% creative offices, and 5% amenities, such as retail. The master plan is both a strategic document and a physical design. It describes the kinds of work spaces, businesses, and institutions the BNY has targeted for growth, pinpoints the location and size of new buildings, and illustrates proposed massing for each of the four proposed projects. In addition, it highlights the concept that already exists in the Yard for vertical industrial development as an innovative building typology that can house quality jobs.

The BNY master plan was the starting point for the students' investigations into how the BNY intends to grow and what it hopes to accomplish as a "leading innovative work-space developer and economic driver for New York City."

The Innovative Urban Work Space

Before considering future development at the BNY, we asked the students to contemplate the character of the urban workplace. With the onset of COVID-19 there had been, and continues to be, considerable uncertainty about its future role. Major companies like Facebook and Twitter have announced the intention to continue encouraging remote work, leaving landlords and developers wondering whether urban workplaces will be needed at all. However, manufacturers and makers continue to require on-site production and distribution of products.

As the studio began, it was too early to tell how the pandemic and changing market forces would impact urban work and how these changes would affect tenants' future rental decisions. It was clear though that the needs and desires of prospective employers and tenants are critical in the design of commercial and industrial buildings. If these conditions are in transition, the buildings designed to house these tenants must change too. But how?

We asked students to consider that the average American worker spends 90,000 hours, or one-third of his/her time, at work. If we believe that work should enhance and support life, then the thoughtful design of our future workplace is a crucial topic to consider.

The design of future work spaces will also have a significant impact on the health of our cities.

According to the United Nations Environment Program, buildings and their construction together account for 36% of global energy use and 39% of energy-related carbon dioxide emissions annually. Therefore the location and design of future commercial and industrial spaces can exacerbate or mitigate the challenges that cities face as they struggle with climate change, aging infrastructure, growing populations, and increasing social and economic inequities. High-density commercial buildings are often the worst offenders. So the studio also focused on how the students' designs for the Yard could contribute to better environmental outcomes.

Finally, in defining innovative urban work spaces students learned that the type of space they propose will influence the types of jobs available. While the BNY and the city acknowledge that there is no looking back to the age of traditional urban manufacturing, the hope is that new work spaces can contribute to creating a more equitable society and a greener environment. This will not happen without a concerted effort by the BNY to target certain types of businesses and support their growth. Thus the students were encouraged to think of the ways architects and developers can consider the factors inherent in building design that affect outcomes for job creation, worker experience, urban equity, and environmental stewardship.

The Site

For the Bass Studio we selected the BNY's Kent Avenue A North site ("Kent A North").

This triangular parcel is located at the northern edge of the BNY, just outside the campus gates. Kent Avenue, a major thoroughfare connecting the Brooklyn Queens Expressway and the Williamsburg Bridge, bounds the site to the north. The Barge Basin, a man-made waterway that leads to the East River, runs along its southern edge.

The site comprises approximately 220,000 square feet of land area. It is zoned M3-1, permitting many industrial and commercial development types but precluding residential use. For Kent A North the master plan proposes development of an 800,000-square-foot building containing a configuration of industrial and office uses that reflect the BNY's ideal tenant mix. Development of a publicly accessible open waterfront space is also suggested.

The Project

The Brooklyn Navy Yard's overarching goal is "to fuel New York City's economic vitality by creating and preserving quality jobs, growing the city's modern industrial sector and its businesses, and connecting the local community with the economic opportunity and resources of the Yard."[2] This objective highlights the purpose of developing buildings at the BNY; however it does not address the complex and often competing physical challenges of a particular site's surroundings or the market conditions that may affect future developer and tenant responses.

We asked students to thoroughly explore Kent A North's context in ways that the master plan does not address and to consider four issues:

1 Is this an appropriate site for industrial use?
2 Is 800,000 square feet an appropriate size?
3 How can the project take advantage of the site's waterfront location to benefit the city, the BNY, and the community?
4 Is there a market (i.e., future tenants) for the proposed uses?

Students identified essential design and development issues presented by the site's location, size, and shape. This led them to contest the program and circulation plan proposed in the master plan. Then the students were asked to devise a mission-driven program to maximize quality job creation while considering a

2 https://www.brooklynnavyyard.org/about/mission

contextually appropriate design for the site's development. Some students found an opportunity in the site's adjacency to the Barge Basin, inspiring ideas for water-based industry. In this way the project became an exploration of the seemingly contradictory demands of the BNY's desire for large-scale development and the severe constraints of the site in terms of both use and access.

Methodology

The studio followed a process similar to that of an architectural development project in three related and overlapping phases:

1 Research, Site Analysis, and Case Studies
2 Program and Project Design
3 Project Presentation

Through a series of research-and-analysis exercises, case studies, and panel discussions with experts during the first weeks of the studio, the students were immersed in the physical, social, and economic issues that frame the site's development. Students had the opportunity to discuss the issues with the leadership and master planners of the BNY as well as with local officials, city planners, and technical experts in the fields of urban design and sustainable building technology. They worked in teams to research and present case studies of precedents and other comparable projects, study different types of urban work spaces, and tackle the questions raised by public and urban waterfront development.

During the research-and-analysis phase, students responded to the development proposal contained in the master plan. After identifying the issues it presented, they explored alternatives for the site's development. They worked toward reconciling the competing demands of the BNY's mission, the site's challenging conditions, the neighborhood context, and financial feasibility. The goal was to devise an optimal development program that would respond to the site's unique conditions while meeting the BNY's mission and objectives.

By midterm each student had developed a project concept supported by analysis, diagrams, design drawings, and a detailed building program. Between midterm and final presentation of the schemes, the students focused on detailing their design concepts to a high level of architectural resolution while testing the logic of the program's mission and feasibility. They also honed their presentation skills to ensure that their narrative and design schemes would carry the intended impact.

Conclusion

"As a nexus of technology, community, and the locus of our livelihood, the workplace is a topic of perpetual interest in architecture and interior design."

— Blaine Brownell, *Architect*, May 2020

For most of us work is a necessity. But for some it is also a privilege. Can the public and private sectors work together to create better job opportunities? Certainly. Can architects who design workplaces create ways to enhance the work experience? Absolutely. Can everyone involved in the development of buildings contribute to new construction technologies that mitigate climate change? We must.

This Bass Studio provided a forum for students to explore how they might improve urban workplaces and help generate quality jobs. The final projects vary significantly in their approaches to fulfilling this public mission. None of the students opted to use the proposed master plan for the design. Instead an exciting array of possibilities were presented, all unified by the conclusion that an 800,000-square-foot development is too large for the site.

The students' speculations and provocations prompt real-life questions about the BNY plan for the Kent North A site. In particular, they highlight the possibility of transferring unused bulk from Kent

North A across the Barge Basin to the site known as Kent North B, which is better suited to industrial use due to its potential for larger floor plates, more truck bays, and safer vehicular and pedestrian circulation. The BNY administration can ponder the students' questions knowing that there will be no loss of floor area or job-creation opportunities because the unused building rights from Kent North A development can be applied elsewhere in the Yard.

Beyond the BNY, these student projects identify interesting new urban business models. They also question the future relationship between places of production and places of consumption, highlighting today's fragile supply-chain issues. Flood mitigation, environmental remediation, and the use of local resources, both physical and social, are other strategies that are applicable elsewhere.

Approaches to commercial and industrial design and development are constantly evolving. The students who participated in the Bass Studio gained insight into how to inform future design thinking by considering every project's specific environmental, program, site, and market parameters.

CONVERSATION

Abby Hamlin and Dana Tang, with Nina Rappaport

The following interview with Abby Hamlin and Dana Tang was published in Yale School of Architecture's *Constructs*.

Nina Rappaport

How did your paths cross in New York, and how did you decide to teach a studio together at Yale?

Abby Hamlin

Our paths crossed in part through Dana's partner, Richard Gluckman, whom I have known for many years because we were both on the board of the Van Alen Institute. He told me that he had asked Dana, whom he described as "a fantastic architect," to become a partner a few years ago. Deborah Berke suggested that Dana teach with me.

NR

How did you decide you wanted to be a real estate developer after studying urban planning at Princeton, and how did development become your passion in a circuitous way?

AH

My first career was as a professional modern dancer, which continues to inform my work as a developer. I have an acute understanding of how our bodies respond to space and how the built environment affects our mood. When I stopped dancing, I was drawn to architecture. But I learned that

architects don't really make all the design decisions; developers do. So I decided to become a developer and use development as a way to create spaces that enhance people's lives. Urban planning was just an intermediate step for me to get into development.

NR

Dana, you too had a circuitous route to a career in architecture. First you taught Chinese and literature at Colorado College, and much later you studied architecture. What inspired you to leave teaching and make this abrupt career change?

Dana Tang

On the one hand it was a very circuitous route, but on the other hand the writing was on the wall. When I was a child I built elaborate villages in the woods, and then as a junior in high school I interned for Prentice & Chan. Lo-Yi Chan advised that I attend a liberal arts college rather than study architecture as an undergraduate. I went even further and pursued a master's degree in Chinese studies. While I was teaching at Colorado College I felt a calling to build things and make space. As an older student at Yale I could bring a broad perspective to my studies in architecture. Ten years later I helped to build our firm's portfolio of work in

Schermerhorn, Polshek Partners Architects

China, which includes three major museums — so things came full circle.

NR

In terms of launching your practice, Abby, you worked for some New York mega developers. How did you know you were ready to be an entrepreneur and start your own firm at a time when there were only a handful of women developers?

AH

Yes, sadly there were only a handful of women when I founded Hamlin Ventures 23 years ago, and it is still the same. Now there are more women coming through the pipeline as real estate executives. I had a desire to be my own boss and decide what projects to work on. But I needed three things to attract lenders and partners: knowledge, capital, and a reputation. I had a really wonderful mentor at Swig Weiler & Arnow, a commercial real estate company that built, owned, and managed office buildings including the Grace Building, in Manhattan, and the Fairmont Hotels. After I became president of that company, I was tasked with selling its entire portfolio. One could say that I was selling myself out of a job, but I saw it as the opportunity I was looking for to strike out on my own. I feel incredibly lucky that I had a vision early on and was able to see it through.

NR

Dana, how did you first team up with Richard Gluckman and later become a partner in the practice with him as a male-female team that is not a romantic partnership as well — which is a little unusual?

DT

Oh that is interesting; I've never thought of that. I first met Richard when he was a critic at Yale and then I had a summer job at Fox & Fowle, where we worked with him on some projects in China. After graduating from Yale I applied to work with him, and I never left. From the beginning I took on a leadership role both on projects and within the office. Richard and I are each other's best critics. We're very complementary. As a female partner there are unique challenges, including the balance between being a mother and a business owner.

AH

You're so right, because part of it was timing: waiting until I felt comfortable with where things were in my home life before becoming an entrepreneur.

NR

The role of gender is also interesting in terms of its impact on cities. There is a community project in Vienna for a housing and neighborhood development initiated by women, where the female gender plays a role in the location of different activities. Do you see cities being built differently from a woman's perspective, in terms of design or ownership structure?

DT

I think women tend to be less egocentric, so the need to make a singular mark is less of an inclination for many of us. I don't think about making a singular object or a big sculptural element that demands attention — I think about the experience of the built environment. For me the individual credit is not as important as everyone working collaboratively as a team to create the best project.

AH

Women developers, like myself, have to operate in a predominantly male real estate system that values money, power, and ego over other objectives. That said, I have found a way to prioritize my goals of creative expression, civic engagement, and design quality so long as my projects earn the same returns as those of any other developer. But it's not automatically gender based. I believe that confident and creative leadership of cities, based on an understanding that all development is a public act, can make a real difference.

NR

Dana, what would you say was your most successful collaboration with a developer, especially in a project where many of the parameters were already established? Where did you find a collaboration that worked especially well for you from the start of the project?

DT

While much of our work is for institutions, we have had a few collaborations with developers, including the hospitality group for whom we designed the Mii amo Spa, in Sedona, Arizona, and we recently completed the Trail House at Enchantment Resort. Hospitality developers are thinking about the guest and the bottom line. Great architecture provides an elevated guest experience by definition, so we really all want the same thing. For Mii amo Spa, we had a heated debate about why the main circulation space had to be 12 feet wide. We dug in our heels, and now there is a 12-foot-high by 12-foot-wide skylighted spine that elevates the feeling of being in the building — and defines the guest experience. The client gained an appreciation of architecture as a way of thinking about spaces as places and not just as program elements related to revenue, and that informs our work together.

NR

How do you relate to the urban context in your projects in terms of community engagement as both outreach and feedback, as well as the physical conditions of the site?

AH

I can't develop anything without being inspired by the context. Even when the context is awful, if I am inspired I can see its potential. A good example is the Hoyt Schermerhorn project, which at first glance was a barren parking lot sitting over the subway across from the criminal courts in Downtown Brooklyn.

Schermerhorn, Interior

Other developers considered this site "unbuildable." I saw it as an opportunity to create a new city block, which is exactly what I did by developing a series of projects including town houses, supportive housing, a theater, and a ballet school. It is now a vibrant cultural hub and mixed-income residential community, anchored by the award-winning 14 Townhouse and Schermerhorn projects.

NR

Dana, is there a project that you feel really represents the way you engage context, site, and community?

DT

Since we don't pick the site, understanding the context is a critical part of our design process. There were two academic projects in the office at the same time that had very different contexts. The Korman Center at Drexel University, in Philadelphia, involved a renovation and addition to what was a 1950s library with an opaque brick face at the heart of campus. Our approach was to open the building, layering the facade from the landscape to the front porch and the atrium. We transformed the sense of place for the community, which was the university. The other project is the Zhejiang University Museum of Art and Archaeology, in China, the first building designed for a new campus in what had been agricultural fields. We had to anticipate the future development of a park and other campus buildings. Our design weaves the landscape between bars of the building, responding to the original landscape and a future built context.

NR

Abby, what have been your most engaging or satisfying projects for nonprofit organizations, and why do you work with them?

AH

I've always sought meaning in my work. It's not that I consider real estate development lacking in meaning, but it is a for-profit endeavor, so I enjoy supplementing that effort by consulting with or serving on the boards of nonprofit organizations. The two areas of nonprofit work that I'm currently focused on are the arts and affordable housing. I've enjoyed working on many projects in these sectors over the years, but I feel particularly proud of the Schermerhorn, with 217 units of supportive housing and a community theater in the base.

NR

Dana, you are really known for your museum clients. What is the best method or the most interesting project you have worked on with a board of directors among these clients, and how do you navigate the art world?

DT

It is a real privilege to have museums and art institutions as our bread and butter, and we can avoid agonizing over whether we are doing this just for money or for a greater purpose. We have had the opportunity to design many first museum buildings for institutions, such as the Georgia O'Keeffe

Gluckman Tang Architects, Korman Center, Drexel University, Philadelphia

Museum, in Santa Fe, New Mexico, in 1997. For the past nine years we have been working with the museum on a new building. Our work goes beyond the design of a building, and we have the ability to better any project with broader interdisciplinary thinking. We try to bring that kind of thinking to every project by asking ourselves what we can do to make a project better in a holistic sense. If you go in a straight line you get one answer, but if you take the time to zigzag around something, you can often find other benefits.

AH

That is exactly the approach I look for in architects — a meandering thinking that takes us to new places. Richard, Dana, and I are definitely going to do projects together!

NR

How did you organize your studio at Yale for a waterfront site that is part of the vital, sustainable, and successful public-private organization of the Brooklyn Navy Yard? And why did you select that particular site?

AH

The Brooklyn Navy Yard is another nonprofit board that I am involved with. Its mission is quality job creation. The site we selected is at the edge of the Yard, so it challenges the students to address issues of the urban context both on the water and inland in the community.

DT

They responded to the mission of the Brooklyn Navy Yard by creating industrial jobs and learned what goes into a feasible economic project. More importantly they contemplated issues of the urban waterfront context to create a project that benefits the city and the neighborhood.

BROOKLYN NAVY YARD'S MASTER PLAN

In 2016 WXY Architects was selected through an RFP process to prepare a master plan that would serve as a blueprint for the Yard's growth and future development. At the beginning of the studio Paul van der Grient, associate principal at WXY, presented the firm's conceptual plan to the class. Johanna Greenbaum, executive vice president of the BNY, and Shani Leibowitz, senior vice president for development at the BNY, joined the presentation. The students were instructed to analyze the plan and be prepared to challenge or defend its conclusions in terms of the studio site. They could then choose whether to use the master-plan program and massing as the basis for their own project design or produce an original program and design, supported by an analysis of the site, to achieve an optimal outcome in the public interest.

Working closely with the Yard's professional team during the planning process, WXY considered the existing conditions, opportunities, and constraints; conducted stakeholder interviews; and developed a physical plan. A summary of the entire plan is available at www.brooklynnavyyard.org/masterplan.

BNY's Strategic Goals

The master plan begins with a "Sector Mix" that defines the types of businesses located in the Yard today. This is followed by a diagram of a tenant "Growth Strategy" that shows the proportion of businesses by type that the Yard hopes to attract through future development. In particular, the master plan targets three manufacturing sectors for 70% of its desired growth capacity: traditional manufacturing, including food, apparel, and garment/textile production; innovative manufacturing, including makers of goods, electronics, prototyping, and technology; and producers for the City of New York, including artisanal production, woodworking, metal fabrication, furnishings, and construction.

To financially support the growth of these three manufacturing sectors, the master plan recommends that 25% of new development be

Sector Mix   **Three Development Sites**

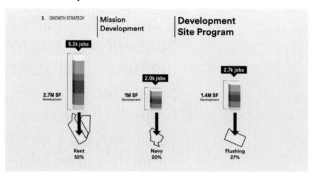

designed as creative office space and 5% be reserved for amenities and services. The total proposed new development for the Yard is 5.1 million square feet distributed across three priority sites on the campus.

Vertical Factories at the BNY

Another goal of the BNY is to build multistoried factory buildings, or "Vertical Urban Factories."[3] As land availability in the Yard shrinks and flooding risk grows due to climate change, the expansion of manufacturing use will depend on the BNY's ability to create new buildings that can lift industrial use above the ground floor, where industry generally prefers to operate. Vertical factory buildings, or "vertical urban factories," is not a new concept here — the Yard already has loft spaces that host production — but it is rarely considered by industrial speculative developers for new construction.

As urban manufacturing evolves away from traditional production practices toward small-scale enterprises, the BNY envisions a return to multistoried buildings. The site already has a significant number, many of which have been renovated. The question is whether new multistoried buildings should be developed speculatively, and if so how should they be designed to provide features that will attract the types of tenants sought by the BNY.

The master plan includes several illustrations portraying the

3 See Nina Rappaport, *Vertical Urban Factory* (Barcelona: Actar, 2015/2020).

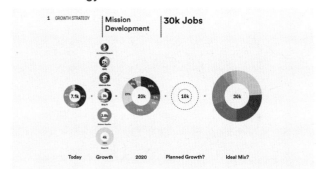

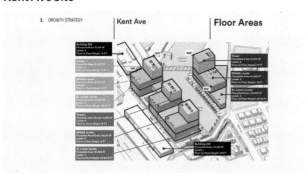

concept of vertical manufacturing drawn from the work of consultant and author Nina Rappaport, whose book *Vertical Urban Factory* is the basis for the BNY's inquiry. This building typology integrates large-scale, innovative, and artisanal manufacturing, along with showrooms and other publicly accessible uses. All of this is situated above the parking and loading facilities of each project, none of which can be below grade at the BNY due to the risk of flooding.

Development Plan for the Studio Site

The Bass Studio focused on the Kent North A segment of the master plan's Kent A Site. The Barge Basin borders this parcel to the south, and Kent Avenue borders it to the north. Out of a total of 1.6 million square feet of development proposed for the entire Kent A site, the northern portion that the students evaluated is slated for a mixed-use building that contains roughly half, or 800,000 square feet. Development of a public promenade around the Barge Basin is also proposed.

The master plan contains a general massing illustration of the proposed development, which is in keeping with the vertical industrial building prototype that BNY hopes to foster. The building base has large floor plates that step up to an 18-story tower on the site's western corner. The program is layered accordingly, with traditional manufacturing located on the second level, above the building's amenity, parking, and loading spaces; innovative manufacturing is slated for the central floors; and creative office space is planned for the tower section. The entire building sits above grade to address the flooding that will inevitably occur.

BARGE BASIN WEST

MAKERS SHOWROOM

MAKERS SHOWROOM

PANEL

Panel Discussions on Urban Planning

As part of the research-and-analysis phase of the Bass Studio we invited four guests — with expertise in planning, design, environmental strategy, and urban waterfront and industrial development — to join us for a discussion of how to achieve the best civic outcomes for the site. We divided the discussion into two parts. First, we had a broad-ranging conversation about goal setting for public land development with Kate Ascher, Justin Garrett Moore, and Andy Darrell. This brought into question the development program presented in the master plan and the fundamental premise that creating "quality" jobs effectively addresses the massive inequities faced by New York City's diverse population. We also discussed the environmental issues inherent in waterfront development and the opportunities presented by the site's adjacency to the waterfront.

Nina Rappaport led the second part of the discussion, presenting her work on the history of the factory and the evolution of industrial architecture, and then introduced her thinking about a new vertical industrial building typology. This new development typology is what the BNY seeks for the studio site and other parts of the Yard.

Kate Ascher

Kate Ascher has authored books about New York City including *The Works* and *Anatomy of a Skyscraper*. She is the Milstein Professor of Urban Development at Columbia GSAPP and teaches courses on real estate infrastructure, the history of development in New York City, and urban planning. In addition, Ascher is a prominent planning and economic consultant whose clients include cities and governments worldwide. She has extensive experience in both public- and private-sector development. She was executive vice president at the New York City Economic Development Corporation and has held positions at the Port Authority of New York & New Jersey and developer Vornado Realty Trust. Ascher is a graduate of Brown University and holds an MS and a PhD in government from the London School of Economics.

Justin Garrett Moore

Justin Garrett Moore is the inaugural program officer for the new Humanities in Place program at the Andrew W. Mellon Foundation. In this role Moore leads the implementation of the foundation's strategic plan for the program, which seeks to highlight a variety of histories and voices in public, media, museum, and memorial spaces and to widen the range of complex public storytelling. He is also working with the foundation's president to shape and lead its Monuments Project — a $250 million five-year commitment to reshape the United States' commemorative landscape. Moore was executive director of the New York City Public Design Commission during the design review of all buildings proposed at the BNY. An architect and urban designer by training, Moore prioritizes the power of public design to help solve significant social challenges. He received degrees in architecture and urban design from Columbia University's GSAPP, where he is an adjunct associate professor of architecture in the Urban Design and Urban Planning programs. He has lectured widely and taught at Yale, Tuskegee, and Morgan State Universities. A member of the American Planning Association's AICP Commission, the Urban Design Forum, and the boards of IOBY, BlackSpace, and the Youth Design Center, Moore is also the cofounder of Urban Patch, a social enterprise focusing on community development and design.

Andy Darrell

Andy Darrell is chief of strategy at the Environmental Defense Fund (EDF), one of the largest environmental nonprofits in the United States, and leads the team focused on urban initiatives. He has developed solutions that combine policy change and private investment, focusing on accelerating investment in clean energy and electric transport, especially in communities that are most vulnerable to the effects of climate change. Darrell was executive director of the Hudson River Park Alliance and wrote the legislation that changed much of the zoning of the Hudson River from manufacturing to parkland. An attorney, Darrell serves on New York City's Sustainability Advisory Board and has served on the boards of many other organizations, including the Van Allen Institute for Public Architecture.

Nina Rappaport

Nina Rappaport is an urbanist, architectural historian, and educator. As director of Vertical Urban Factory, a think tank and consultancy, she focuses on the intersection of production spaces, architecture, and the role of the factory worker. She is the author of *Vertical Urban Factory* (Actar, 2015; 2nd ed., 2020) and curator of the eponymous traveling exhibition. Rappaport edited the book *Hybrid Factory/Hybrid City* (Actar, 2022), a collection of essays based on a conference in Torino, Italy. She coedited *Design for Urban Manufacturing* (Routledge, 2020) and *Industrial Palimpsest: Newark, N.J.* (Actar, 2022). She lectures internationally and has published essays in numerous journals. As Publications Director at the Yale School of Architecture, she is editor of the magazine *Constructs*, the studio book series, and exhibition catalogues. She has been a visiting professor at the Politecnique of Turin and Sapienza University of Rome. She is also coordinator of history/theory of architecture at the School of Public Architecture at Kean University.

The Questions

The questions posed to the panelists emerged from the students' analyses of the master plan in terms of the site and context. They understood the conflicting forces faced by a developer in selecting an optimal program and building design. Although the purpose of the site's development is to support the public mission of the BNY — to create the maximum number of "quality," mostly industrial, jobs — the location and shape present significant challenges for industrial use and for developing a large-scale vertical industrial building. The site also offers an opportunity to consider its adjacency to a waterway that connects to the East River:

> Would supporting a water-dependent use add value to the project?

> Could the site's development mitigate environmental issues such as flooding and sewer overflow?

> Could the site's design take advantage of its location as the terminus of the Williamsburg waterfront promenade?

We sought the panel's insight on how a developer might grapple with the challenges and opportunities of the studio site given its ownership by the BNY and whether a future developer could successfully propose a project whose public goals and merits differed from those currently sought by the BNY. If so, what might those other public objectives be? We also asked panelists to consider the vertical industrial building typology and to comment on the appropriateness of the building concept shown in the

master plan, calling for an 800,000-square-foot building to house modern manufacturing and creative offices.

Discussion One: Public Development Goals

Optimal public benefit is an imprecise, abstract goal for developing a building on publicly owned land: It is not the building itself that produces public welfare but tenants and taxes. So determining what should be built is a question of who would occupy a building and why. Some excerpts from the discussion reveal the gist of the panelist's varied responses to how a developer might select public objectives for the site.

Kate Ascher

"One thing I can say for New York City is that it is almost impossible to develop affordable manufacturing space on privately owned land in Brooklyn and, increasingly, in Queens. The fact that the public sector has land available for manufacturing development that may create jobs for individuals most in need has to be privileged over other goals."

Justin Garrett Moore

"We have to push on that point because the sad reality is that it is simply not true that for people of color industrial jobs are necessarily a path to economic equity. We need to go a little further into that conversation. Jobs are important, and we should be producing jobs. But who really benefits from these jobs? What is the diversity of the jobs produced? If this project does not create real opportunity for the people most in need, then we cannot suggest that developing new industrial work space at the BNY is an adequate public goal.

"Furthermore, we need to look at what makes a neighborhood and a community thrive. The BNY is surrounded by three massive public housing projects and other residential communities. What are the resources and infrastructure that the surrounding communities need? We need to combine our understanding of new industrial production, the benefits of job creation, the physical requirements of new production facilities, and the local context in which they will be situated. Planning, designing, and engaging around the local community's needs rather than working within the little box of maximizing industrial job production is a more inclusive strategy, and in the long run it will provide a greater resource for the people of the city as well as the city economy."

Andy Darrell

"The notion we all agree on is that this public site must be developed for the public benefit. But what public benefit? We do not know who the tenants of a speculative building will be until the building is occupied. This means you must design today for something that will benefit the city and its people tomorrow without knowing what kinds of jobs will be provided and for whom. If job production becomes a primary goal of this project, I still would like to see you set some other public objectives.

"As an environmentalist I see a few big trends that the Environmental Defense Fund is asking all of our stakeholders, companies, and governments to engage with as public benefits when they are

making development decisions. One of those is the significant global imperative of climate change. How can your design for this site help NYC deal with climate change? Second, there is the issue of environmental justice. What is the local environmental impact of your project? Will the project you propose bring additional truck traffic, noise, and air pollution into the surrounding community? How is the community helping you figure out what this site should be? What amenities might you provide to enhance the connection between the site and the neighborhood? Consider the impact of development on the biodiversity of the site and the city. Adjacency to the water is both a challenge (flooding) and an opportunity. There are many innovative things happening in terms of water uses in New York, such as growing oysters, floating swimming pools, and restorative wetlands to enhance biodiversity. Battery barges are being placed on waterways for backup power during emergencies and electric-powered water transport. As you select your public goals, do not ignore the water and the environmental and economic possibilities for enhancing your project's civic outcomes."

Discussion Two: Local Context Versus Citywide Objectives

While the BNY has determined that developing an 800,000-square-foot building for modern manufacturing and creative offices will provide the "optimal" public benefit by creating jobs, panelists wondered, Is this really the case? We discussed how to select an "optimal" set of public benefits in the framework of the following issues: Can a speculatively designed manufacturing and office space on this unusually shaped site function well enough to attract the tenant mix that the BNY seeks? Is the size of the public subsidy needed to build this project commensurate with the public benefit it will yield? Should potential negative impacts on the local community be projected and addressed?

All the panelists agreed that job creation is a legitimate public goal. However, not every panelist favored this as the ultimate goal for the studio site, especially not at the proposed scale. Panelists suggested that even if some manufacturing occurs there, students should consider other public objectives to enhance the impact of their projects.

Kate Ascher strongly supported the BNY's objective. She believes that the citywide goal of creating new affordable manufacturing space is increasingly important and difficult to achieve elsewhere in the city. She was not deterred by the site's limited vehicular access or the project's potential to increase traffic, air, and noise pollution in the local neighborhood. She explained, "Today's urban industry is not the polluting industry of the past. New technologies, new environmental standards, and new methods of transport mean that we need not separate industry from residential neighborhoods as the zoning previously required. Appropriate industrial tenancies can coexist within communities without creating substandard living conditions for the residents."

Justin Moore agreed that urban manufacturing has changed and that we need to "unpack" what we mean by industrial development on the site. However, he did not conclude that industrial development is necessarily the optimal or sole public benefit to target for the site. Moore questioned whether job creation through development is the best, and most economically efficient, way to serve the segments of the city's population most in need. He distinguished between job versus wealth creation, noting that the latter must be the city's goal in addressing racial inequities. Moore recognized the importance of local impact even when a project has an essential citywide objective. He hopes to see this site's development establish better connections between the local community and the BNY, possibly by creating ground-level spaces to showcase local artists and companies. He also considered unsafe vehicular circulation and added pollution from increased truck traffic as unacceptable outcomes for the project. Moore weighed in on the question of the waterfront by asking the students to go beyond conventional thinking, namely a park. "You know I love parks," he said, "but not everything needs to be a park. This goes back to the question of what is a public need and how can development of this site impact that need. I think this is key. Should a developer propose a project that will benefit individuals at a local, city, regional, and even global scale? This site is large and well located enough for a developer to propose a variety of public objectives, not just one, at many different scales."

Andy Darrell challenged the students to consider what environmental goals might be achieved along with other goals. Ascher concurred: "I think it is legitimate to ask if the existing footprint of the Barge Basin is where the water should be, and how should we treat the basin? What purpose could this edge serve that it is not currently serving? Must it be an edge, or should it be filled in? There's no reason why we should not be thinking about different ways to use this and other NYC waterfronts."

Although the panelists agreed that job creation is a supportable public objective for New York City, they did not find it to be an adequate single objective for the site. The efficacy of job creation depends on the types of industry and jobs created. "If the jobs we are creating do not provide real opportunities for people, ownership in particular, then you are creating cogs, not jobs," Moore concluded.

Furthermore, the panelists agreed that job creation is insufficient to justify the specific development proposal outlined in the BNY master plan. They objected to that proposal on several grounds: (a) The site's context and shape necessitate vehicular access that crosses pedestrian and bicycle paths; (b) The site has insufficient truck loading and circulation space; (c) The project's floor plates are suboptimal for manufacturing use; (d) Truck traffic will increase noise and air pollution in an already affected neighborhood; (e) The site's adjacency to the Barge Basin is not sufficiently considered; (f) The project's estimated cost ($380 million) is too high for the public benefits it proposes to yield.

These discussions with expert panelists freed students to imagine outcomes that would mitigate problems they had already identified in the master plan as well as envision broader goals for contributing to the public good.

Discussion Three: Vertical Industrial Building Typology

The BNY's goal is "to become an innovator in the creation of vertical industrial spaces," a building type that has existed in cities for many years. Multitenant industrial buildings were essential centers for urban manufacturing in New York City, and prime examples still exist in Soho and the Garment District. Over time these buildings have been converted to other uses, such as office and residential, as industries have relocated elsewhere.

Nina Rappaport, our guest speaker, is a proponent of what she has termed the "vertical urban factory," which can be reintroduced into cities to provide a work space for the needs of today's manufacturers. She has consulted with the BNY, entrepreneurs, and city planning and economic development offices about her ideas for designing and developing this renewed architectural type. We asked her to discuss the typology, its history, form, and purpose, and why it is vital for the BNY to employ these buildings, which are rarely developed in the private market. Finally, we asked her to comment on the appropriateness of a vertical industrial building on the studio site given the context and constraints.

"The Vertical Urban Factory is a multistory loft building that can house manufacturing either fluidly throughout the building or floor by floor, as in a mixed-use production facility. It is more sustainable because workers can live nearby, and by rising vertically the buildings occupy a smaller footprint."

"The BNY site is complex because although manufacturing was once everywhere it is segregated through modern Euclidian zoning regulations, which are necessary for some companies. But I propose that we can mix today's manufacturing, which is primarily small, clean, green, and quiet, including light industries and craftspeople, along with housing, community, and social services to harness the qualities of Industry 4.0. With high-tech machinery and artisanal and small-batch production we don't always need large industrial spaces, and higher-cost uses can subsidize others.

"Historically many factories are designed so that the flow of the industrial process follows the architecture. Efficiency is still a profit motive. In the Modernist era we saw factories like Van Nelle, in Rotterdam, Lingotto, in Turin, and Ford, in Detroit, where both mass production and the factory itself epitomized Modernism. During World War II we had to move factories out of the cities and build them in blacked-out sheds so they would not be detected and attacked from the air. This typology inspired the shed factories of suburbia as well as export processing and industrial zones. In these places we remove the worker from our view, and they effectively lose rights and the ability to fight for better wages. But today's companies have an interest in design, and I have identified five themes for new factory models — the flexible, the sustainable, the spectacle, the commons, and the hybrid. These typologies serve new industries that we see as the Fs — food, fashion, furniture, and fabrication — along with some legacy companies, among others.

The BNY fits into these definitions as host to many companies that prototype smaller things and are high tech, such as those at New Lab.

"A factory space with the potential to reorganize allows a company to be more resilient, with spaces like BLDG 72 in the BNY and Greenpoint Manufacturing Design Center. These can also offer a kind of commons of Fab Labs and maker spaces that help start-ups on the business side or to function like the Hotels Industrielles in Paris, with courtyards to remove truck deliveries from neighborhood streets. The sustainable factory can be closed loop and energy producing, and the mixed-use or hybrid factory can blur the boundaries of use both at the district and the building scale for interconnected ecosystems. The mixed-use factory is rising, for example, Strathcona in Vancouver includes housing and production and the Shinola factory in Detroit, which inhabits a former GM building. New York could require industry as a use in new buildings for light production and evaluate them using what is called "performance zoning" rather than imposing blanket zoning regulations.

"So how do we create this new flexible and sustainable hybrid, and is it really appropriate for the BNY? Perhaps we can learn from the burgeoning field of industrial symbiosis, where at the neighborhood scale interconnections between companies, whether recycling or producing, can create a new paradigm that allows the urban factory to thrive with equity."

SITE STUDIES

Initial Research and Site Studies

In the first half of the studio students worked in teams to research the site's history, edge and access conditions, and surrounding building typologies as well as tenants and occupants of the Brooklyn Navy Yard. The students presented this information at the midsemester review as a framework for the analysis and design of the BNY site.

Physical Conditions of the Site

Over the last 250 years the shoreline and ecology of Wallabout Bay, site of the BNY, has been transformed radically to accommodate a range of water-oriented transportation and urban and industrial activities, as illustrated by the 1766 Bernard Ratzer map overlaid with the current BNY footprint. Located at a crook in the East River, much of the bay was originally saltwater marsh. Repeated dredging, landfill, and hardening of the edges produced the complex environment we see today.

Because of this history of low-elevation landfill and hardened edges, any development of waterfront sites at the Brooklyn Navy Yard requires careful measures against flooding, which will be exacerbated by climate change and sea-level rise. An examination of the FEMA's Sea Level Rise Maps for the 2050s shows the hundred-year flood plain expanding significantly throughout the City of New York. Properties in the flood zone have increased from 24,000 structures in 2010 to 85,000 in 2013,

especially along the Brooklyn waterfront. More than 42,000 structures in Brooklyn are identified as at risk, compared to only about 6,000 buildings previously. Almost all of the Brooklyn Navy Yard will be within that 1% annual flood height line.

The inland urban-edge condition of the Brooklyn Navy Yard, where it meets the adjacent city, balances security control and public access. To the west and south of the Yard, the Brooklyn-Queens Expressway (BQE) separates the BNY from the downtown Brooklyn and Fort Green residential neighborhoods. Warehouses are located across Flushing Avenue in between the BQE and the Yard. To the east of the BNY, residential communities adjoin the Kent Avenue site. There are four security gates, three tenant entrances, and three public entrances. Adjacent to Kent Avenue, at the intersection of Clymer Street, is a gate separating the recycled shipping-container wall erected by Steiner Studios. The newly renovated Building 77 encompasses one of the largest public-entry points from Flushing Yard but has controlled access into the site.

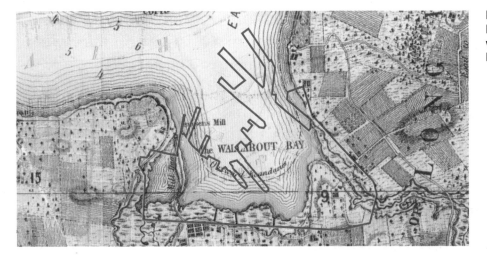

Navy Yard
Boundary Overlaid
with 1766 Bernard
Ratzer Map

2050s Flood Map

Year 2050
Projected
Sea-level Rise

**Kent A Site
Section 1:
Manhattan on
the Other Side**

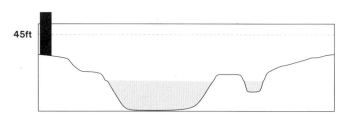

45ft

**Kent A Site
Section 2:
Dry Docks and
Warehouse
Buildings**

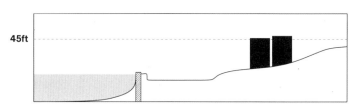

45ft

**Kent A Site
Section 3:
100-foot-tall
Residential
Buildings to the
East**

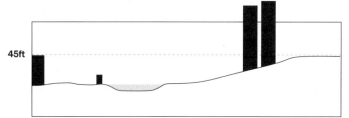

45ft

**View of the
Barge Basin**

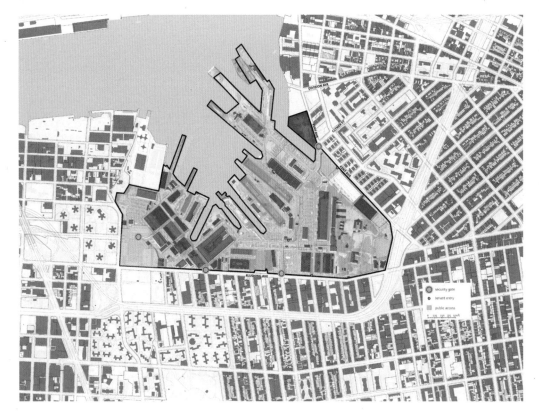

**Brooklyn
Navy Yard Entry
Analysis**

**Steiner Studio
Periphery Wall**

The Innovative Urban Workplace

Steiner Studio

**Clymer
Street Gate**

**Steiner Studio
Periphery Wall**

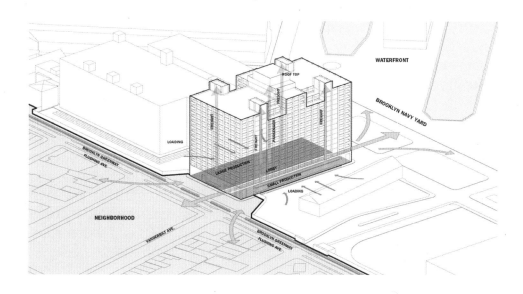

Site Access and Circulation

The Yard offers free shuttle services for those coming from Dumbo (connecting to A, C, F trains) or from Atlantic Terminal (connecting to G and LIRR trains) on weekdays. However, the Kent A site is one of the farthest points from the Atlantic Terminal, and the shuttle does not have a nearby stop. The closest stop on the Dumbo shuttle line is at Railroad Avenue. The Yard is easily accessible via the subway or the Astoria Ferry Line, which stops at the Yard's Dock 72. Employees can take numerous subways that connect with the free Yard shuttle, and by bicycle it takes 5 to 8 minutes from the main MTA stops to the Brooklyn Navy Yard. The Yard has created a bike-friendly environment with racks located throughout for employees and registered visitors. The experimental Optimus Ride autonomous vehicles transport ferry-bound passengers on a continuous loop between Dock 72, Building 77, and the Cumberland Gate. The Kent A site is separated from the rest of the Navy Yard by a congested intersection at Clymer Street, one of the four largest entry points, where the convergence of car, truck, bike, and pedestrian circulation around the Kent Avenue site poses challenges for planning and design.

Occupants

Profile and Projects According to the Pratt Center's Report of 2013

Over the past 100 years, manufacturing at the Yard has evolved from the large-scale production of ships to small-scale artisanal and custom production. Boutique manufacturing firms require proximity to clients for more customized mass production. The Yard also hosts major companies that produce goods from military fatigues to bagels, employing proprietary systems, technologies, and techniques that require the high degree of security in the Yard.

These factors define a high value-added manufacturing sector in New York that represents a new model of urban production. Its products are harder to manufacture abroad, and its jobs are difficult to export. The high degree of value-added production makes company owners willing to pay higher rent and wages because these factors of production consume a lower proportion of total revenue than in traditional manufacturing, where margins are extremely thin.

There are currently 264 direct tenants at the Yard, approximately 25% of which have one or more subtenants, for an estimated total of 330 firms. The BNY also has four city agencies as tenants —a vehicle tow pound, a wastewater treatment plant, a Department of Sanitation salt pile, and the Fire Department's Marine Division—that have been located there since the 1970–80s and account for approximately 15 acres.

Loading Streets

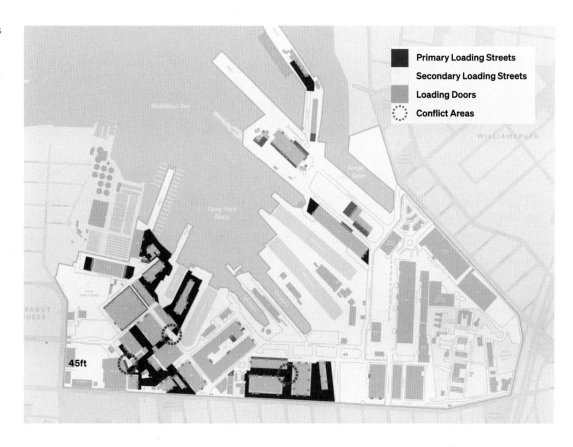

Legend:
- Primary Loading Streets
- Secondary Loading Streets
- Loading Doors
- ⚬ Conflict Areas

45ft

Types of Accessibility

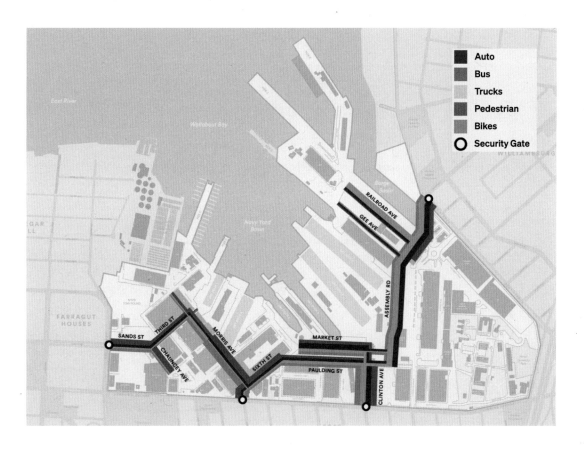

Legend:
- Auto
- Bus
- Trucks
- Pedestrian
- Bikes
- O Security Gate

RAILROAD RD
GEE AVE
ASSEMBLY RD
SANDS ST
THIRD ST
MORRIS AVE
CHAUNCEY AVE
SIXTH ST
MARKET ST
PAULDING ST
CLINTON AVE

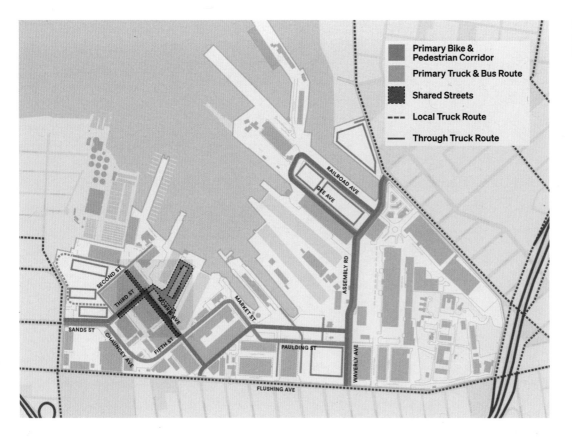

Legend:
- Primary Bike & Pedestrian Corridor
- Primary Truck & Bus Route
- Shared Streets
- --- Local Truck Route
- — Through Truck Route

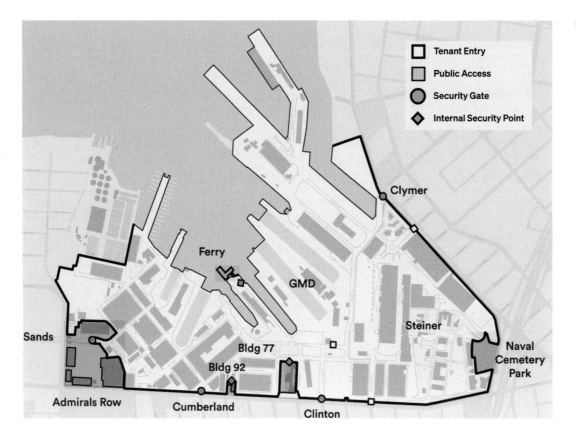

Legend:
- Tenant Entry
- Public Access
- Security Gate
- Internal Security Point

Clymer

Ferry

GMD

Steiner

Naval Cemetery Park

Sands

Bldg 77

Bldg 92

Admirals Row

Cumberland

Clinton

The overwhelming majority of companies fall into the artisanal and/or niche manufacturing category, followed by warehouse and distribution firms.

By the study of 2013, artisanal production made up the largest cluster in the Navy Yard, accounting for 52% of all surveyed tenants and ranging in size from one-person fine-art studios to larger firms with 80 employees. A total of 41% of firms work in the architecture and design industry, 16% in TV production-related enterprises, and 10% in the category of graphic designer and mixed-media artists. A growing community of the surveyed tenants falls in the "green" category, producing green products or incorporating green principles into service delivery.

Intra-Yard Interaction

Part of the BNY's mission as an economic incubator is to encourage interaction between tenants and synergies between industries. According to a 2013 study by Pratt Center for Community Development, 61% of companies at the BNY reported doing business with other companies in the Yard.

The majority (88%) of Yard tenants are selling goods and services in New York City, comprising an average 71% of total sales, and 21% of surveyed firms are selling exclusively within the five boroughs.

Armed with a detailed knowledge of the BNY's physical, environmental, economic, and social conditions as well as its history, students endeavored to develop critical proposals positioned in the next evolution of the Yard. Who would be the most relevant group of tenants addressed by the Kent A site? The research helped the students form an understanding of both the physical condition of the site and the requisite program and scope of the design for their projects.

STUDENT WORK

IVES BROWN

Navy Yard Workforce Development Center

This project uses the position of the site as a unique opportunity for the BNY to interface with the public and the waterfront while fulfilling its mission to create quality job opportunities. The program centers on creation of a workforce training center and a restorative wetland park that infills the neighboring Barge Basin. The proposed workforce-development center expands on the BNY's existing workforce-development initiatives, including the existing STEM center for high school students and a concept for an adult workforce and job placement center.

This new workforce training center will have a specialized curriculum that focuses on producing green infrastructure. Created in partnership with the city university system, it will serve adults seeking to enter the workforce for the first time or be retrained to work in an expanding industrial field. The curriculum will be project rather than classroom based, offering vital hands-on skill development to individuals that the BNY and the City seek to reach.

The training-center design reflects its pragmatic collaborative curriculum. The proposed building contains 110,000 square feet on six levels organized around two distinct types of training space: studios and classrooms. The studios are placed on the north side of the building to provide diffuse light and direct access to roof terraces overlooking the East River with views of the Manhattan skyline. The south tower contains the classroom spaces. The terraced organization of the building follows the new landscape, with wetland green space acting as a terminus to the public waterfront promenade and a working example of how natural infrastructure systems can help deter sea-level rise and flooding. A split in the center of the massing connects a public waterfront promenade to Kent Avenue, providing open community access to the restorative waterfront park. By opening the buildings to the landscape and the public, a gateway is created between the BNY and the immediate community it seeks to serve.

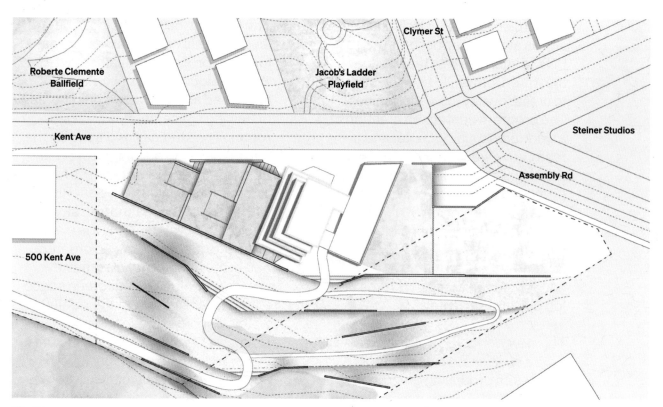

Site Plan

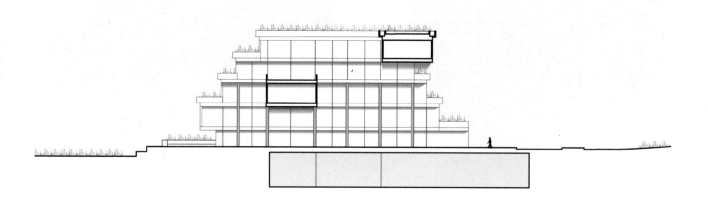

Site Section

The Innovative Urban Workplace

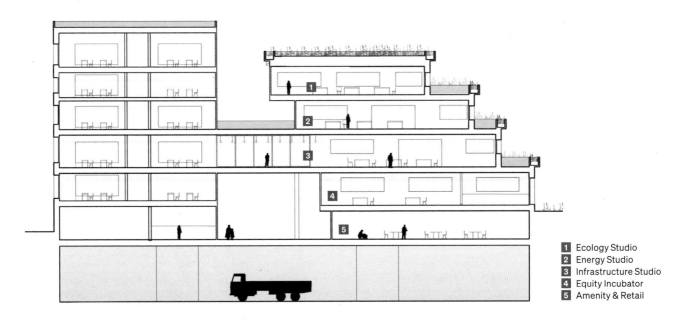

Sectional Relation of Programs

1 Ecology Studio
2 Energy Studio
3 Infrastructure Studio
4 Equity Incubator
5 Amenity & Retail

Interior View

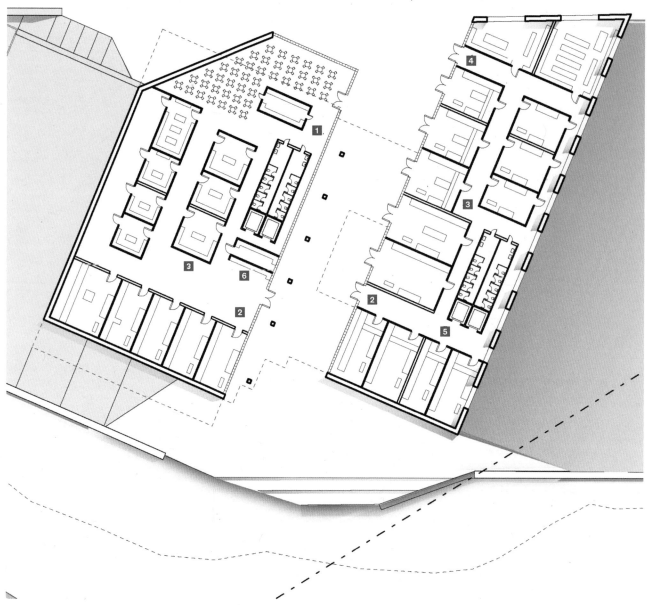

Ground-Floor Plan

1 Café/Restaurant
2 Amenity Shops
3 Showrooms
4 Exhibition Spaces
5 Restroom & Service
6 Entrance Lobby

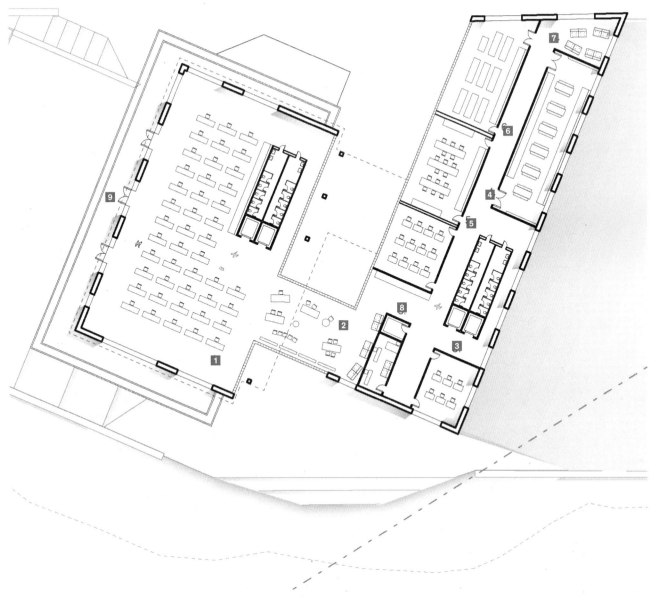

Third-Floor Plan

1   Workshop/Studio Space
2   Multipurpose Space
3   Classroom
4   Fabrication Lab
5   Seminar Room
6   Computer Lab
7   Reading Nook
8   Admin Office
9   Exterior Terrace

View from the Barge Basin

View Corridor

Sectional Relation of Programs

XUEFING PU

Join the Yard

This proposal is for a mixed-use project that combines business offices, community centers, art and music studios, and urban public space. The campus contains three buildings comprising 444,256 square feet of commercial and community space. This reflects a floor area ratio of 2.86, which is higher than that permitted for the site on a stand-alone basis but lower than the 4.96 FAR proposed for the site in the master plan.

The project's varied program and size respond to the site's position at the northern edge of the BNY, adjacent to Brooklyn's Williamsburg residential neighborhood. The project's goal is to connect the BNY with the surrounding community and the greater Brooklyn workforce by offering a comprehensive community-based program that brings energy and activity to the site.

The project design focuses on creating new types of work space that serve as catalysts for interaction among people of different professions. For example, the business tower is designed as a vertical ecosystem that contains both training spaces and job opportunities. The community center connects to the art studios, enabling artists and community members to intermingle both in a classroom setting and in a studio environment. A garden-like podium, lifted above grade, unites the program and the site while mitigating the risk of flooding. In addition, lifting the podium allows a service area below for vehicular circulation.

This community-based approach foregoes the BNY's emphasis on industrial use since the site's limitations are significant enough to suggest that industrial use would be better located elsewhere in the BNY. This site would have its own purpose related to building a connection between the BNY, the local community, and Brooklyn's cultural economy.

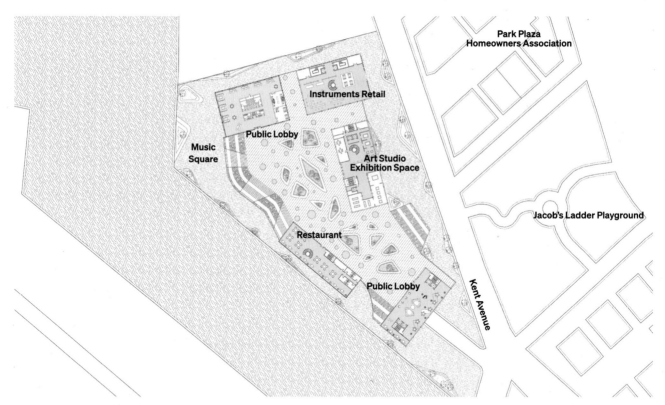

First-Floor Plan

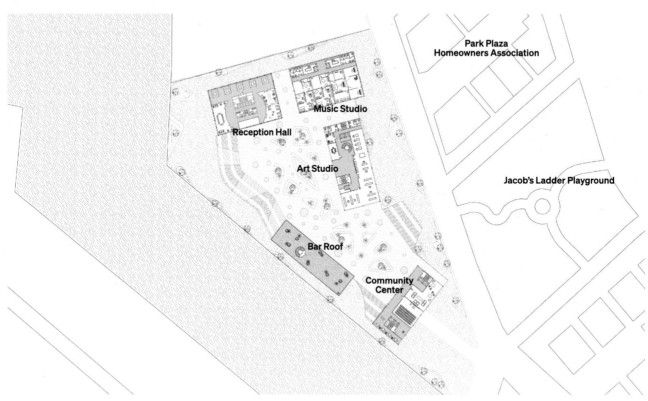

Second-Floor Plan

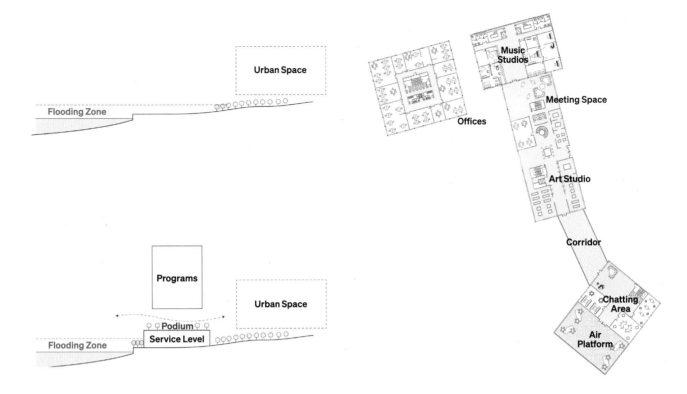

Flooding Diagram

Typical Floor Plan

View to Downtown Brooklyn

View from the Brooklyn Navy Yard

View Looking Into Site From Jacob's Ladder Park

View from the Podium

View to Downtown Brooklyn

NIMA JAFARI

Brooklyn's Innovation Hub

The recent pandemic exposed an inequity of access to parks and work space in Brooklyn's impoverished neighborhoods. This project addresses the issue by creating the Kent Avenue Innovation Hub ("the Hub"), featuring a publicly accessible landscape and a campus populated with communal and private maker spaces and flexible tenant suites. The project will encourage local business development, educate an aspiring workforce in Brooklyn, and serve the community.

The Hub will house a community of creative small businesses and light manufacturers. Unlike traditional manufacturing buildings with large floor plates, the Hub offers multiple pavilions of varied sizes for light manufacturing start-ups to create businesses and share a new work lifestyle that encourages collaboration and socialization by like-minded entrepreneurs. Second Muse, an existing Brooklyn-based collaboration agency, is the kind of company that could operate the Hub and offer communal maker spaces specializing in wood, textiles, and digital technology to accelerate and support the growth of Brooklyn start-ups and advanced manufacturing entrepreneurs. Work and financial training will ensure the sustainability of small businesses and help them scale up.

The Hub's design blurs the boundary between public and private space. Internal courtyards and a proposed esplanade on the ground level welcome employees, pedestrians, and visitors. Local Brooklyn brick and steel define the facade and capture the neighborhood's industrial character and heritage. The massing features a bar typology with three-sided window exposure to Manhattan skyline views and outdoor balconies for many work spaces, designed with open layouts suitable for coworking.

The Hub's hybrid model of making, learning, and sharing will benefit Williamsburg and Brooklyn as a multiuse community outpost. The public-campus scheme allows tenants to exhibit and sell products on the ground floor and scale up their businesses with artisan studios along Kent Avenue. The second floor allows users to access the maker space for textile, wood, and digital technology to enhance their skills. The third floor provides business offices and studio spaces for rent, encouraging budding entrepreneurs to start enterprises. The fourth floor provides an entirely open plan that can be rented to small businesses as they grow.

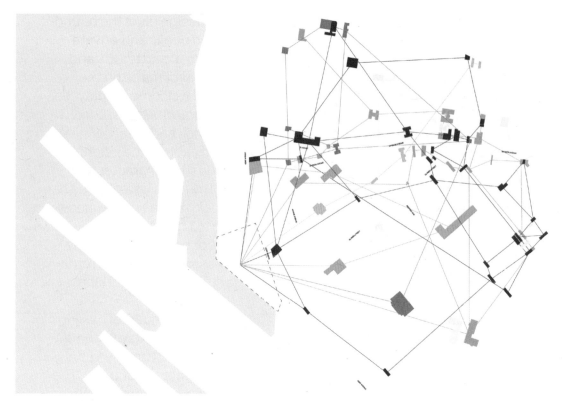

Network: Small Business

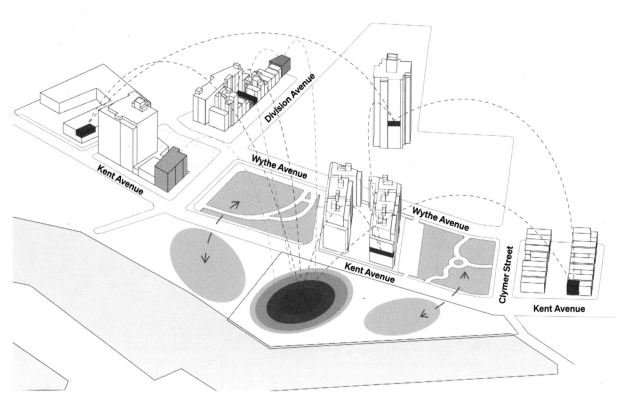

Diagram: Connecting to Small Businesses

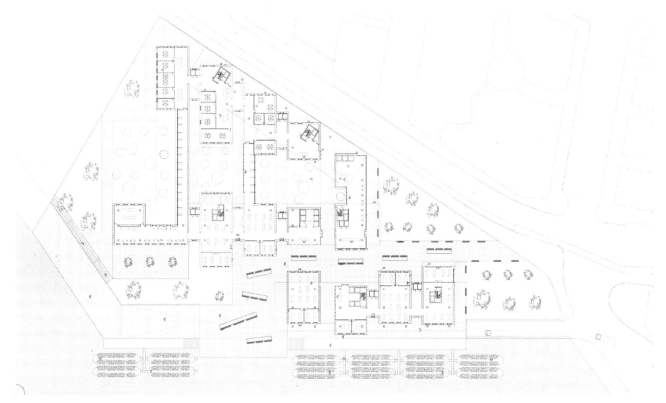

Ground-Floor Plan

Short Section

From Williamsburg Esplanade Barge Basin

Render Facade

Esplanade Terrace Bridges

Inside Bridge-Encapsulated Courtyard in Bar

Kent Avenue Street View

Maker-space Woodshop

HYUN JAE JUNG

The Innovative Urban Workplace

The design of new work spaces must respond to many factors, including rapidly changing technologies and modes of mobility. Spatial, cultural, technological, and systemic changes that affect how we occupy commercial space will continue to evolve in the wake of COVID-19. Thus the next generation of commercial developments must consider whether existing design trends will remain viable or new design ideas will better serve tenants' needs and desires.

This project imagines a design approach for a future workplace model.

Building upon in-depth research on the historical and global paradigm shifts in work spaces and lifestyles, the project suggests a design that will cultivate linkages and interactions between ideas, investments, education, culture, and people. Triggered by the simple idea that proximity to open space will be an important determinant of future success for commercial buildings, the design highlights the use of balconies, terraces, and other open space to create work environments that feel like living rooms and creators' studios outfitted with new technologies.

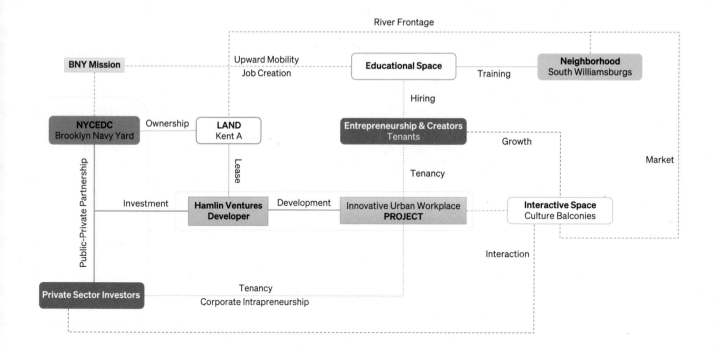

Innovation and Ideas

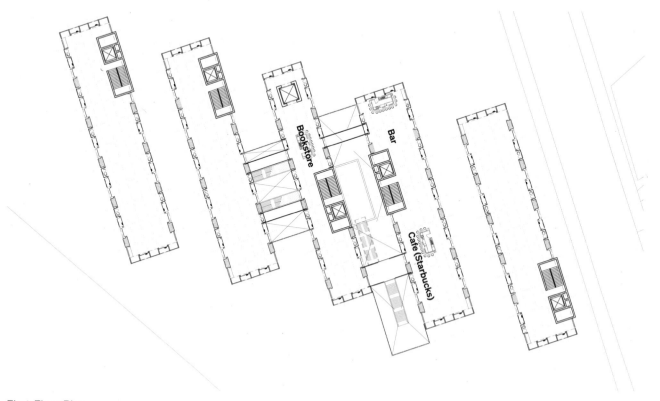

First-Floor Plan

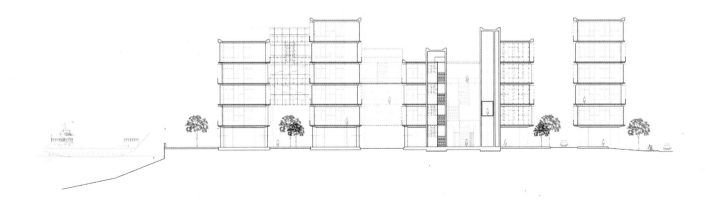

Building Section

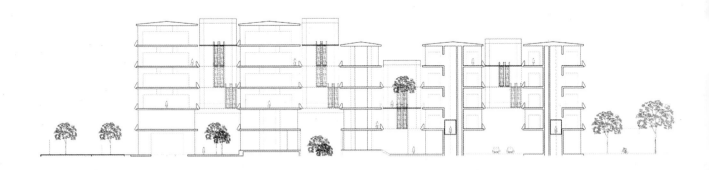

Building Section

Elevation

Atrium

The Innovative Urban Workplace

Site Visual

Internal Street

DREAMA SIMING LIN

Grow, Eat, Learn — BNY Water-Based Educational Farm-Scape

The project intends to reconnect New Yorkers with food sources and promote an innovative soilless water-based food-production cycle. The BNY communal "food-scape" is a laboratory for food production, a marketplace, and an eating destination. It will demonstrate how urban agriculture can be seamlessly integrated into cities and communities by serving both local residents and New York's professional chefs and growers with a facility that reduces the environmental impact of food production and transport.

The project contains a total of 234,350 square feet of building area, accommodating a food-scape program divided into three categories: production (100,500 square feet), consumption (73,850 square feet), and education (60,000 square feet). The massing strategy intertwines these areas so that the farm-scape production area overlaps with the public consumption and education spaces. This spatial configuration reduces the travel distances for the food and creates both an actual and a psychological link between producers and consumers. As visitors get access to fresh produce coming directly from the farm, they will become aware of growth cycles and less dependent on long-distance shipping and trucking for their

food supply. The educational program aspires to revive the local economy on a neighborhood scale by providing training and creating new quality jobs.

In terms of site access, the elevated bike route and walkway separate the traffic flow of automobiles, pedestrians, and bikes for both efficiency and safety. The bikeway above the edible water garden provides cyclists with an enjoyable didactic experience. Pedestrians can access the site either from the waterfront promenade or from Kent Avenue. Both entry points open into a central courtyard that contains a farm-scape and a farmer's market. This public space will also be available for community activities such as concerts, performances, and yoga classes.

By applying intensive water-based growing methods, the project converts the waterfront site into a highly productive public asset where the community can grow food, eat, and learn while reducing the need for polluting food transport. By achieving the BNY's goal of job creation through a communal food space this project achieves a dual public purpose: it accomplishes employment growth and expands our collective awareness of innovative urban agriculture techniques that improve the environment.

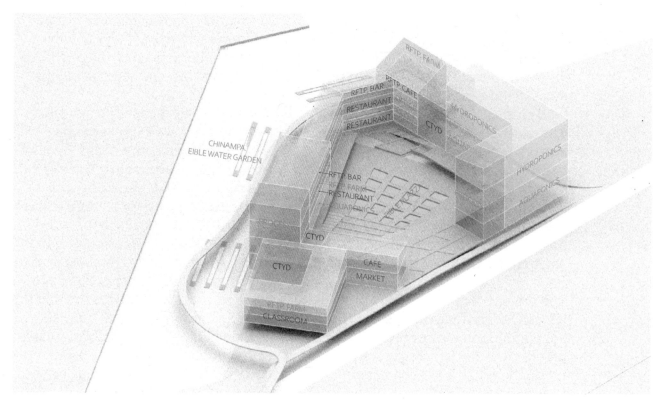

Massing and Program Diagram

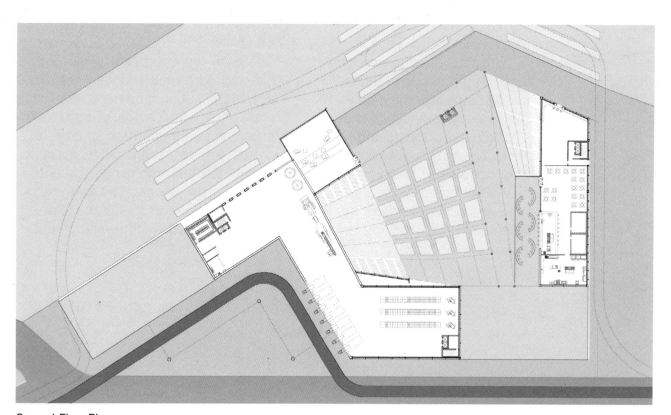

Ground-Floor Plan

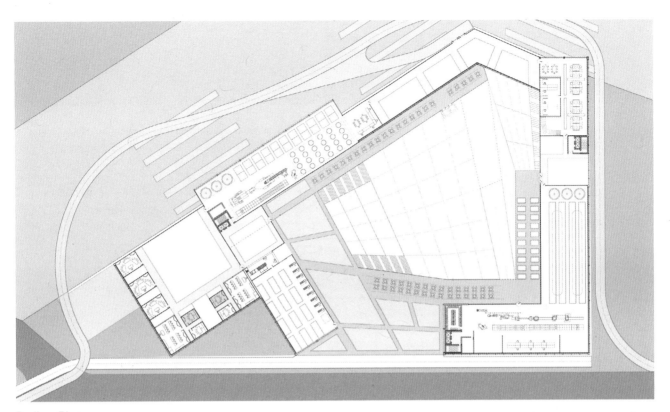

Podium Plan

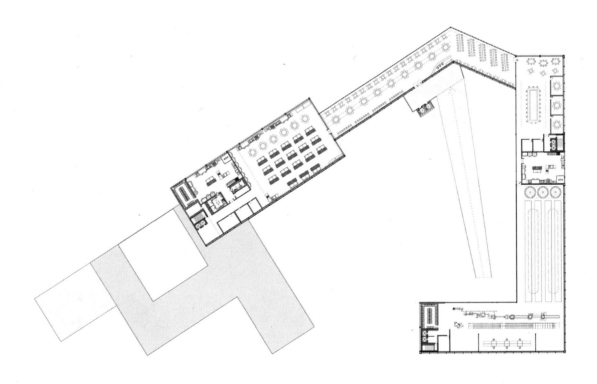

Rooftop Plan

Facade on the Waterfront

View of the Market

The Innovative Urban Workplace

STELLA X

Urban Food Hub at the Brooklyn Navy Yard

This project introduces a new food-production and retail model that reflects the reality of e-commerce and post-pandemic urban food production, consumption, and research while supporting Brooklyn's employment needs by adding new industrial, service, and laboratory jobs. The result is a publicly engaging, experiential, environmentally sustainable food hub and dietary research center for New York City that concentrates food production on-site, including farming, manufacturing, processing, cooking, distribution, and retail.

As the site is sandwiched between the Brooklyn Greenway Initiative and the future waterfront promenade, which connects the South Williamsburg Ferry Station and the Clymer Gate, the project separates truck and car access from bike and pedestrian routes. An elevated bike path allows logistics vehicles to pass underneath, on the ground level, enhancing rider safety.

The design of this 180,000-square-foot project negotiates between the opposing spatial qualities of the artificial vertical farming shafts toward Kent Avenue (production and work) and the absence of buildings toward the Barge Basin (communal, leisure, landscape). Three modes of urban agriculture coexist on the site: an indoor vertical hydroponic farm, a productive landscape that could serve as community gardens facing the waterfront, and an aquaponic farm on the barges. Most of the interior public programs are concentrated around the ground floor. A seasonal garden market and open kitchen connect the interior to outdoor farming spaces, which could host temporary events led by chefs or sustainable food and farming classes. Work spaces for production, processing, distribution, and offices are arrayed on the upper levels.

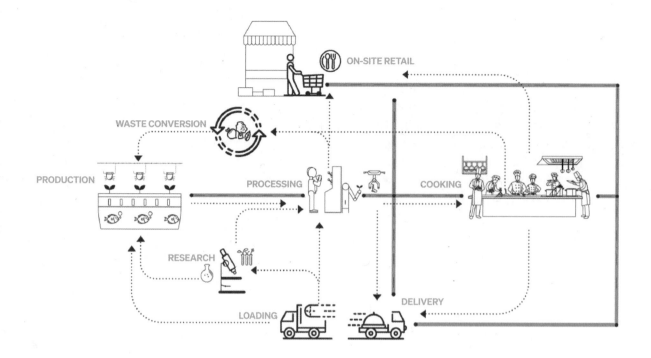

ON-SITE RETAIL

WASTE CONVERSION

PRODUCTION

PROCESSING

COOKING

RESEARCH

LOADING

DELIVERY

From Production and Processing to Distribution

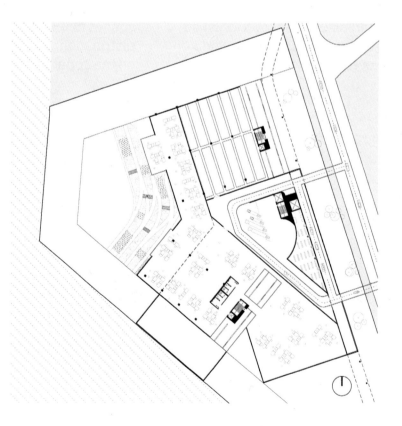

Ground-Floor Plan

Podium Plan

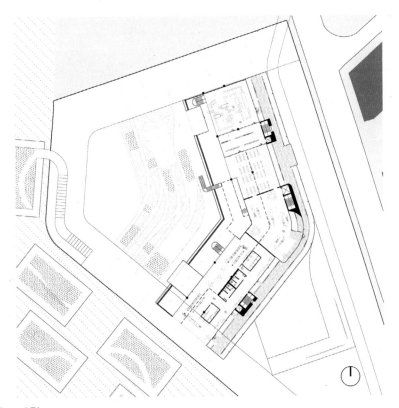

Office and Production-Level Plan

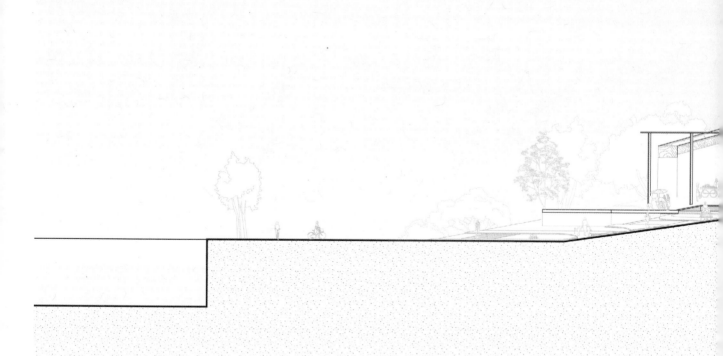

Building Section

Elevation on Kent Avenue

The Innovative Urban Workplace

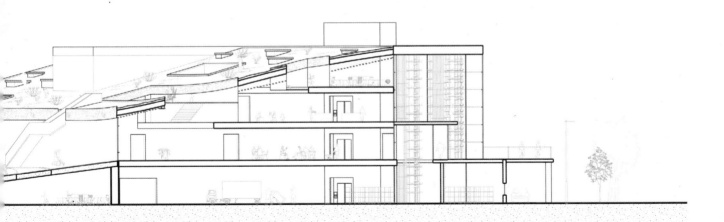

View of the Garden Market

YOUNG JOHN YUN

The Innovative Urban Workplace

The Brooklyn Navy Yard has adapted to its stakeholders' changing needs over time — first a young country at war, then a nation with a booming economy, and finally a municipality striving to retain industrial jobs. The BNY's evolution often struggled against a fixated vision of spatial use or antiquated spaces that were no longer viable.

Today the BNY's waterfront programs are relatively inactive. This project seeks to recapture the vibrant use of the waterfront by creating an oyster habitat in the Barge Basin. Research into the oyster's internal and external form and functionality led to the project's proposed design, in which the building form closely aligns with the creature's ovular shell and core gill structure. The result is a multistory factory within horizontal networks of trade, a low-rise context, and cultural amenities that will make the project self-sustaining.

Based on the idea of using the oyster's biological reproduction cycle, the 150,000-square-foot building will hold three innovative programs: oyster harvesting, industrial tourism, and rainwater protection. By implementing this oyster ecosystem program, the Barge Basin will become a rich, diverse, and abundant estuary that helps to clean the East River, into which it leads. The communities surrounding this complex new ecosystem will help construct it and, in return, benefit from sustainable cycles of opportunities for work, education, and recreation.

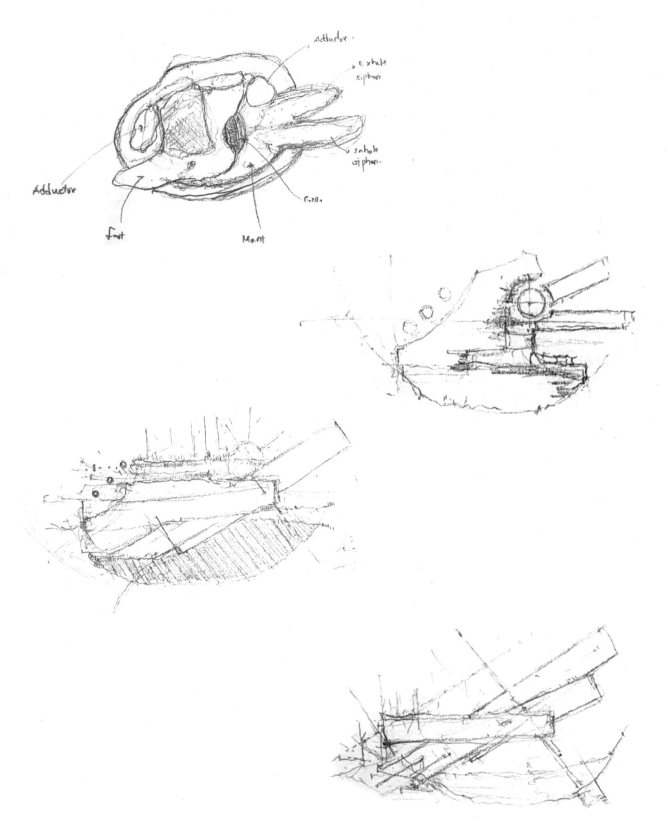

Design Inspiration Sketches: Biological Forms

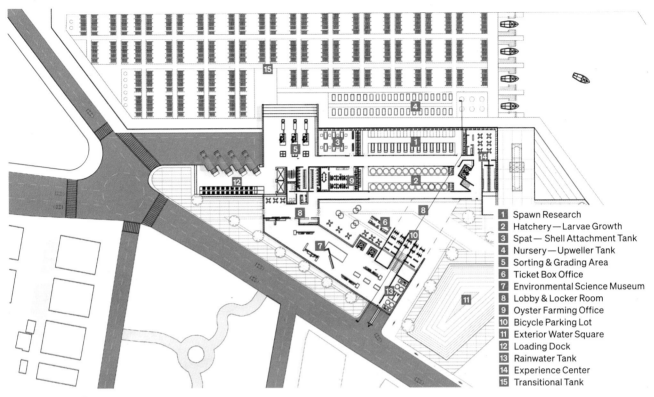

Ground-Floor Plan

1 Spawn Research
2 Hatchery — Larvae Growth
3 Spat — Shell Attachment Tank
4 Nursery — Upweller Tank
5 Sorting & Grading Area
6 Ticket Box Office
7 Environmental Science Museum
8 Lobby & Locker Room
9 Oyster Farming Office
10 Bicycle Parking Lot
11 Exterior Water Square
12 Loading Dock
13 Rainwater Tank
14 Experience Center
15 Transitional Tank

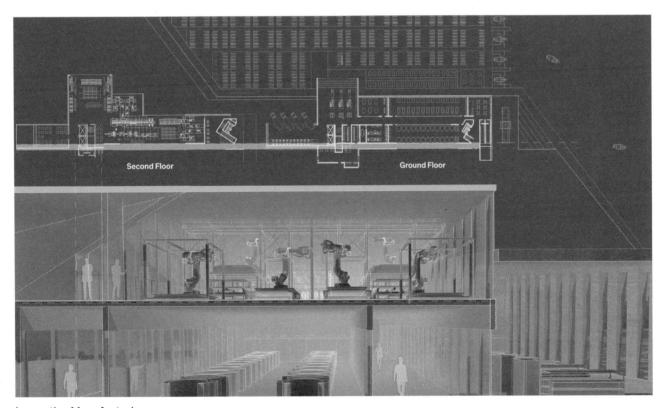

Second Floor   Ground Floor

Innovative Manufacturing

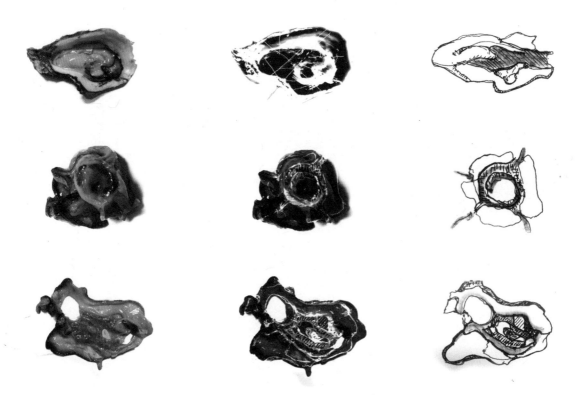

Oyster Anatomy Diagrams

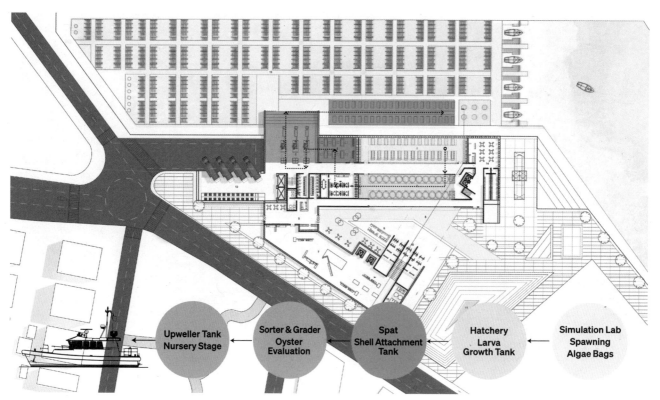

Oyster Farming Diagrams

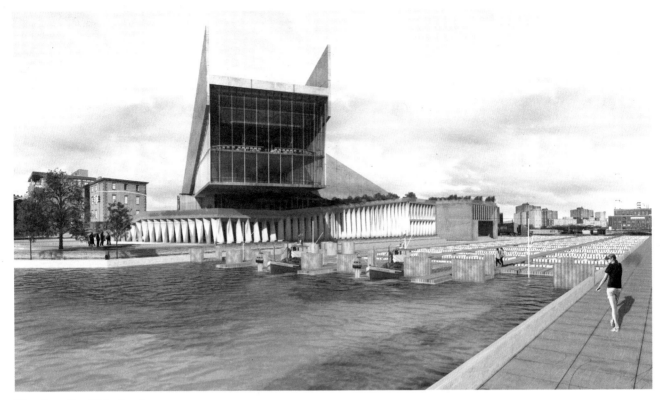

View from the Waterfront

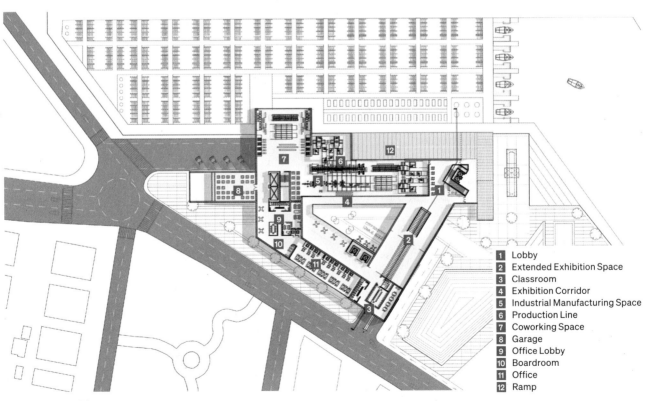

1 Lobby
2 Extended Exhibition Space
3 Classroom
4 Exhibition Corridor
5 Industrial Manufacturing Space
6 Production Line
7 Coworking Space
8 Garage
9 Office Lobby
10 Boardroom
11 Office
12 Ramp

Second-Floor Plan

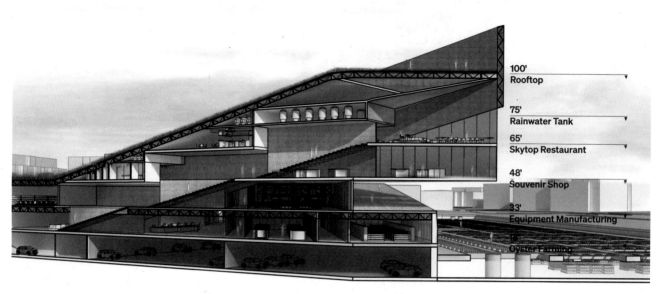

100'
Rooftop

75'
Rainwater Tank

65'
Skytop Restaurant

48'
Souvenir Shop

33'
Equipment Manufacturing

Oyster Farming

Building Section

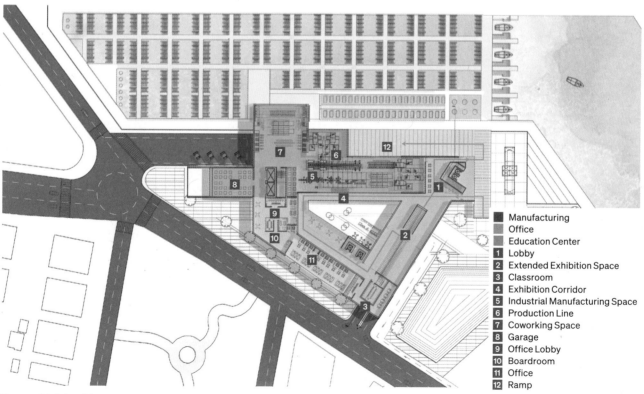

- ■ Manufacturing
- ■ Office
- ■ Education Center
- **1** Lobby
- **2** Extended Exhibition Space
- **3** Classroom
- **4** Exhibition Corridor
- **5** Industrial Manufacturing Space
- **6** Production Line
- **7** Coworking Space
- **8** Garage
- **9** Office Lobby
- **10** Boardroom
- **11** Office
- **12** Ramp

Space-Division Diagrams

Farming Barges

Skytop Restaurant

YUHAN ZHANG

E-boat Central — Toward the Next Decade of the Brooklyn Navy Yard

The historical identity of the shipyard vanished with the decline of water-based transport in the city after World War II. This project aims to carry the Yard's dual legacy as a mecca for shipbuilding and innovative technology by creating a sustainable center on the site that showcases the technology and manufacture of e-boats. It will also serve as a tourist hub for visitors eager to see how new technology is used to create e-boat prototypes and small-batch manufacturing.

The 169,600-square-foot building is organized around an assembly line that showcases the prototypes from cutting-edge research through development. Other programs — including an auditorium, a cafeteria, an exhibition space, and offices along the assembly line — interact to provide a diverse and lively new community center.

The dynamic form funnels all the movement around the e-boat manufacturing activities. A soft edge responds to the site's boundaries with a prominent facade on the waterfront and a low profile along the neighborhood street. The sawtooth roof brings sunlight into the deep plan of the open space, which transcends the conventional manufacture-showcase dichotomy and reminds people of the manufacturing gene of the Brooklyn Navy Yard.

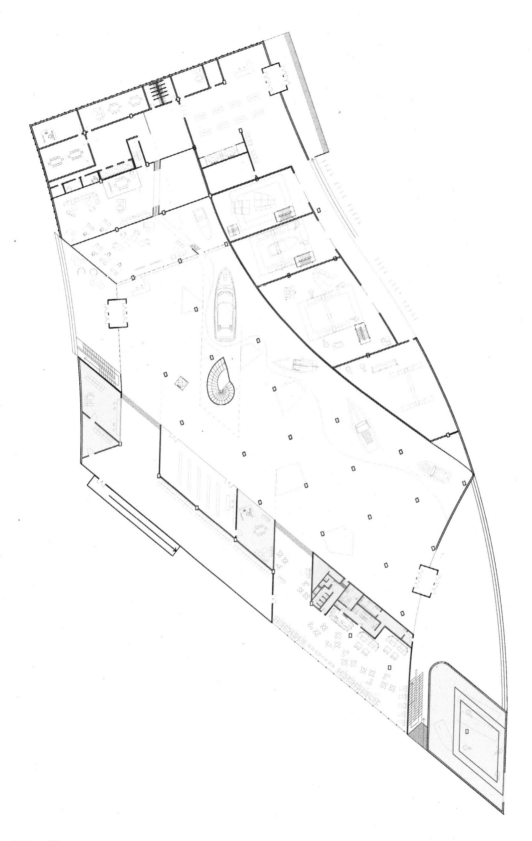

Ground-Floor Plan

The Innovative Urban Workplace

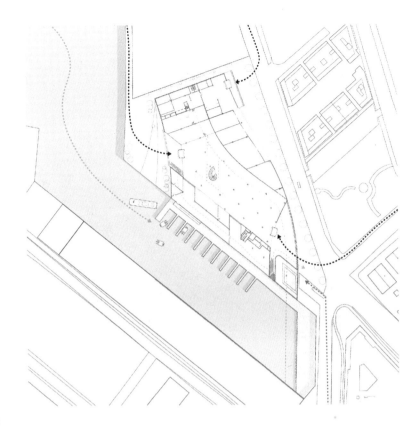

Section Perspective

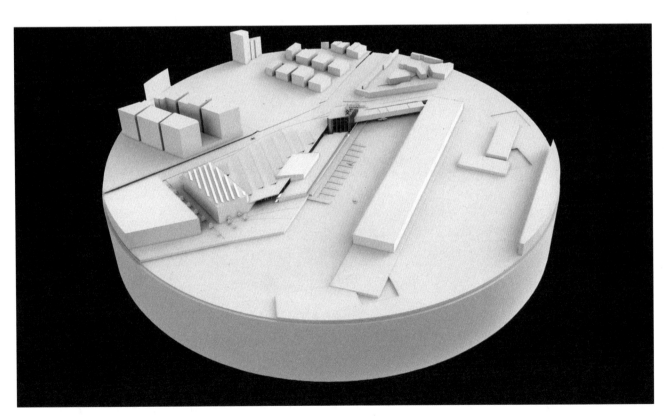

Site Model

Section Perspective

View from the Waterfront

The Innovative Urban Workplace

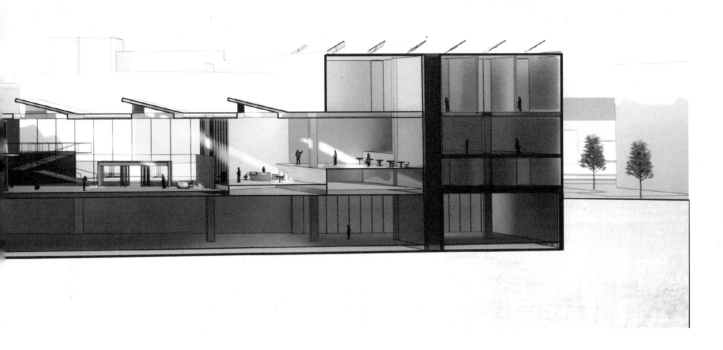

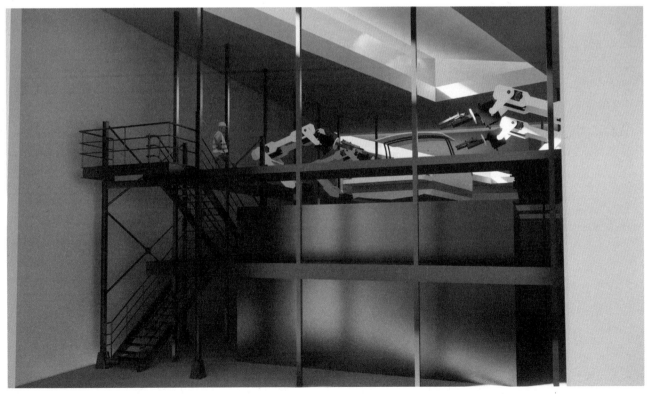

Boat Production

Image Credits

Andrei Harwell: 20, 21, 27

David Sundberg: 30, 33

Bruce Damonte: 33

Dreama Simeng Lin: 52–53, 54 (bottom), 55 (top and middle), 96–101

Hyun Jae Jung: 88–93

Ivcs Brown: 64–69

Marvel Architects: 55 (bottom)

Niema Jafari: 80–85

Rogers Marvel Architects: 35

Stella Xu: 54 (top), 104–109

WXY Architecture for Brooklyn Navy Yard: 38 (top), 39 (top), 40–41, 57, 58

Xuefeng Du: 72–77

Young Joon Yun: 112–117

Yuhan Zhang: 52, 53, 120–125